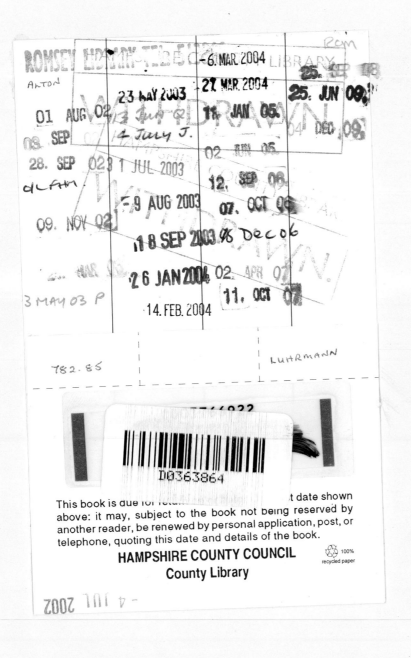

This book is due for return by the last date shown
above: it may, subject to the book not being reserved by
another reader, be renewed by personal application, post, or
telephone, quoting this date and details of the book.

HAMPSHIRE COUNTY COUNCIL
County Library

100%
recycled paper

THIS STORY IS ABOUT
FREEDOM

1.

Vou - lez - vous couch - er av - ec moi____ ce - soir?____ Vou - lez - vous couch - er av - ec moi?__

2.

N.C.

____ 2. He Vou - lez - vous couch - er av - ec moi.____ *Spoken:* He come

through with the money and the garter-belts, let 'em know we got their cake straight out the gate. We

independent women, some mistake us for whores. I'm saying why spend mine when I can spend yours?

Disagree? Well that's you and I'm sorry. I'm - a keep playing these cats out like Atari, wear

high-heeled shoes, get love from the Jews. Four bad-ass chicks from the Moulin Rouge.

Hey sis - ter, soul sis - ters; bet - ter get that dough, sis - ters!

Spoken: We drink wine with diamonds in the glass by the case, the meaning of expensive taste. We wanna

3. Touch of her skin_ feel-ing silk-y smooth,_ col-our of ca- fé au lait._

(Verse 4 see block lyric)

Made the sa - vage beast_ in - side_ roar un - til he cried_ More!_

2° D.%. al Coda   ⊕ **Coda**

_ More!   More!_

Vou - lez - vous couch - er   av - ec   moi_

_ ce soir?_   Vou - les - vous couch - er   av - ec   moi?

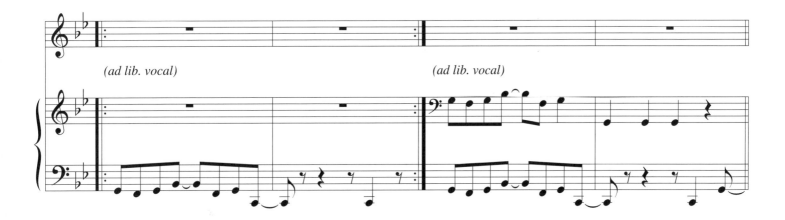

(ad lib. vocal)   *(ad lib. vocal)*

Play 4 times

(ad lib. vocal)   Cre - ole La - dy Mar - ma lade.

molto rall.

Ooh,   yes - sa!

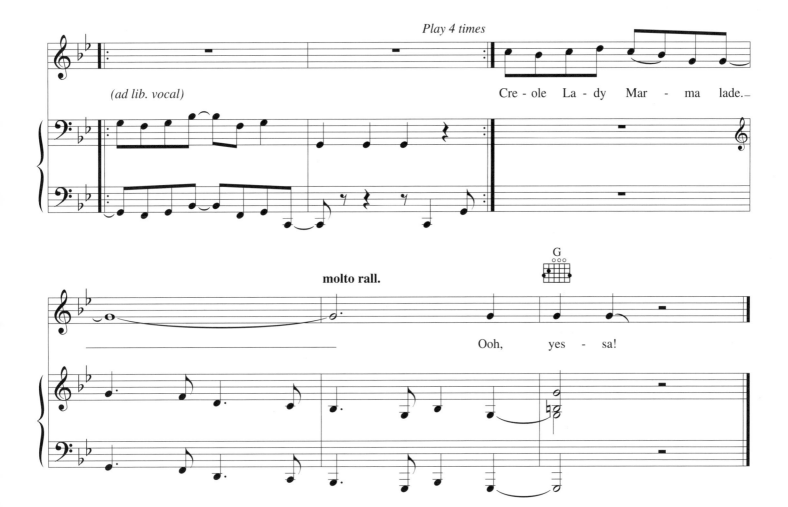

Verse 2:
He sat in her boudoir while she freshened up
Boy, drank all that magnolia wine
(All) her black satin sheets
Swear he started to freak, yeah.

Verse 4:
Now he's back home doing nine to five
Living a grey-flannel life
But when he turns off to sleep, memories keep…
More! More! More!

BECAUSE WE CAN

WORDS & MUSIC BY NORMAN COOK

Ho - ho.⎯ Ho - ho.⎯ Ho - ho.⎯ Ho - ho.⎯

Ho - ho.⎯ Ho - ho.⎯ Ho - ho.⎯

Ev - 'ry - bo - dy can - can. You can can, can, can. You can can, can, can. You can

can, can, can. Be-cause we can can - can. Yes, we

can can-can.   Yes you can, can, can, can, can, can, can, can,   can, can, can, can, can, can, can, can.

Ho - ho.___   Ho - ho.___   Ho - ho.___   Ho - ho.___

1.

N.C.

Ho - ho.___   Ho - ho.___   Ho - ho.___   Ev-'ry-bo-dy can - can!

2.

N.C.

Yeah, yeah, yeah, yeah, yeah, yeah, yeah, yeah.   Yeah,   yeah,___   yeah,___   yeah,   yeah,   yeah,___

yeah,—— yeah, Yeah, yeah,— yeah,—— yeah, yeah, yeah,—

yeah,— yeah, Yeah, yeah,— yeah,—— yeah, yeah, yeah,—

Drums, percussion

Ho - ho.___ Ho - ho.___ Ho - ho.___ Ho - ho.___

Ho - ho.___ Ho - ho.___ Yes we

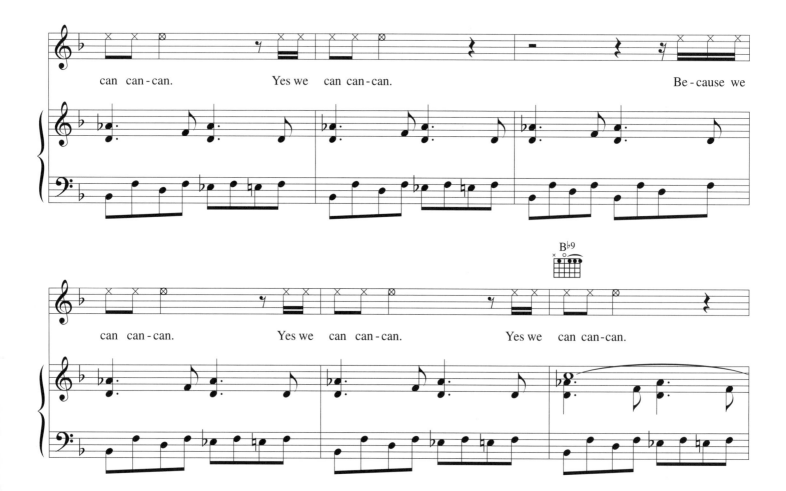

can can - can. Yes we can can - can. Be - cause we

can can - can. Yes we can can - can. Yes we can can - can.

17

SPARKLING DIAMONDS

SEE PAGE 88 FOR COMPLETE SONG TITLES AND WRITER/COPYRIGHT DETAILS

The French____ are glad to die____ for love,

A kiss on the hand may be

quite con - ti - nen - tal but dia - monds are a girl's best friend.

kiss may be grand but it____ won't pay the ren - tal on your hum - ble____ flat____ or

help you feed your __ pus-sy cat. Men __ grow cold as __ girls __ grow old and we all lose our charms in the

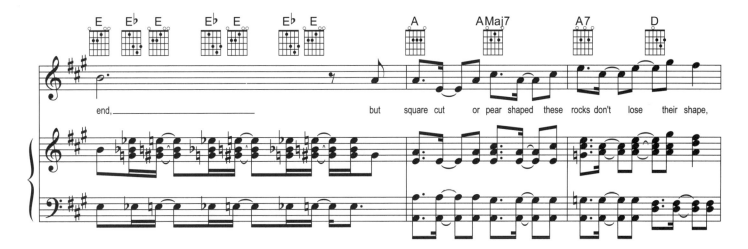

end, _____ but square cut or pear shaped these rocks don't lose their shape,

dia-monds are a girl's best friend. Tiff-a-ny,

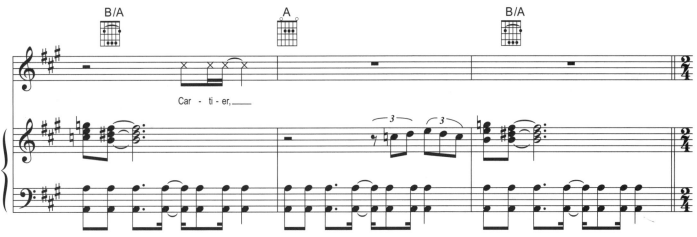

Car - ti - er, ___

19

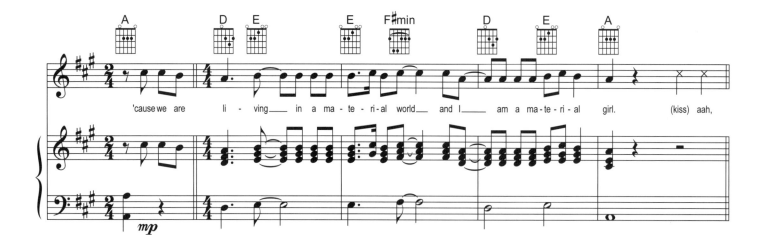

'cause we are li - ving____ in a ma-te-ri-al world____ and I____ am a ma-te-ri-al girl. (kiss) aah,

come and get me boys.

There may come a time when a lass needs a law - yer,____ but

dia-monds are a girls best friend. There may come a time when a hard - boiled em - ploy - er thinks you're

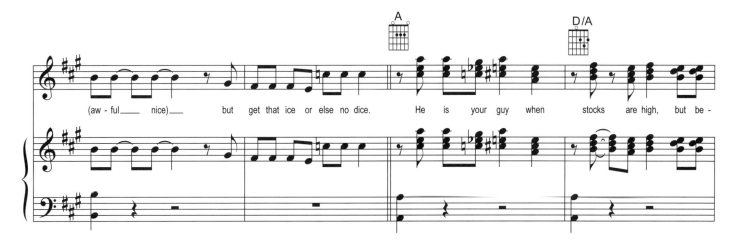

(aw - ful___ nice)___ but get that ice or else no dice. He is your guy when stocks are high, but be -

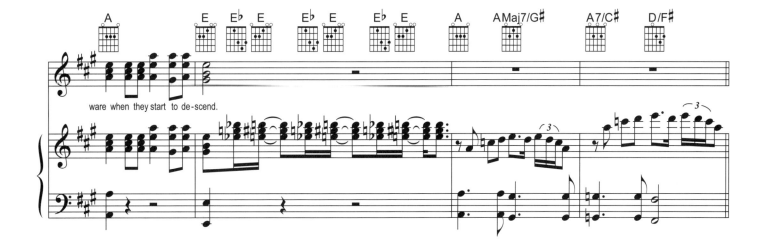

ware when they start to de-scend.

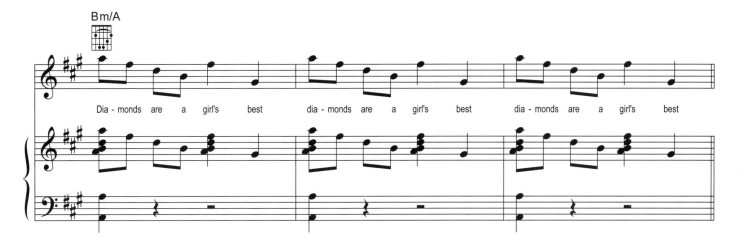

Dia - monds are a girl's best dia - monds are a girl's best dia - monds are a girl's best

friend.

(Sample Break)

'cause that's when those lous - es___ go

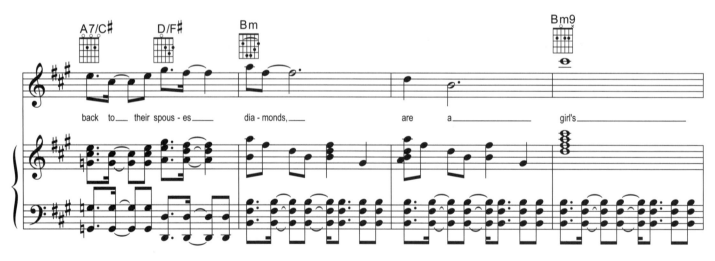

back to___ their spous - es___ dia - monds,___ are a___ girl's___

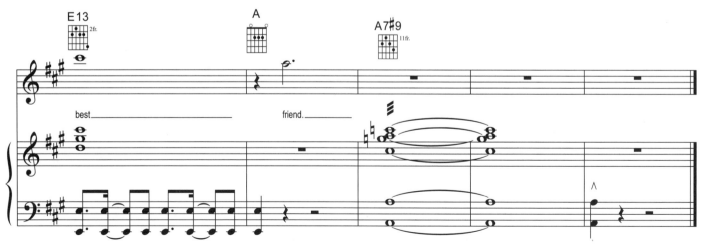

best___ friend.___

RHYTHM OF THE NIGHT

WORDS & MUSIC BY DIANNE WARREN

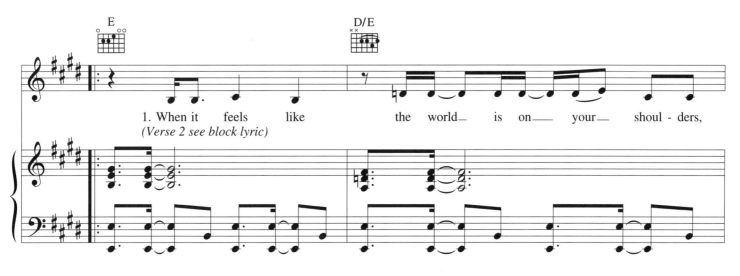

1. When it feels like the world— is on— your— shoul - ders,
(Verse 2 see block lyric)

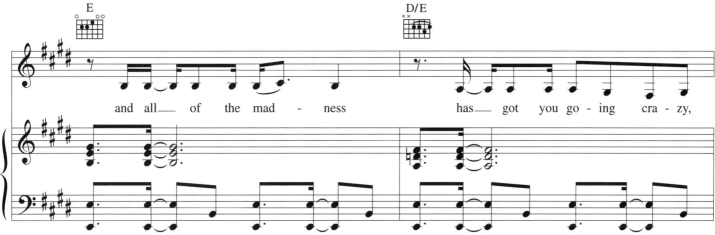

and all— of the mad - ness has— got you go - ing cra - zy,

it's— time to get— out, step out— in - to— the— street

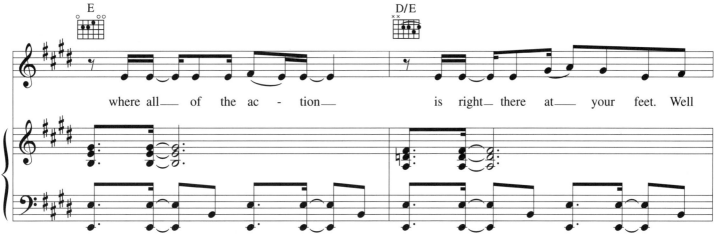

where all— of the ac - tion— is right— there at— your feet. Well

(Get the beat of the rhy-thm of— the night.) Dance un-til the morn-ing

light. (For-get a-bout the wor-ries on— your mind.) We can leave them all— be-

-hind. (Get the beat of the rhy-thm of— the night.) Oh, the rhy-thm of— the

night. (For-get a-bout the wor-ries on— your mind.) We can leave them all— be-

27

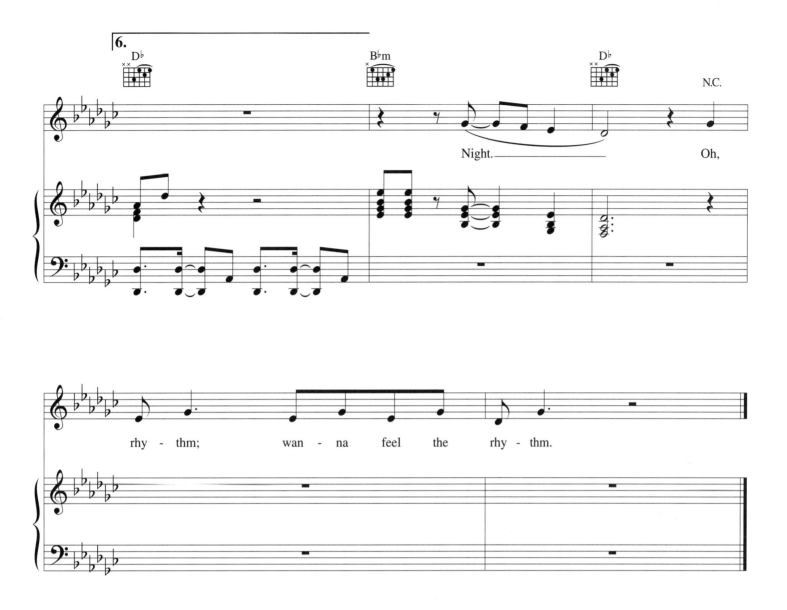

Verse 2:

Look out on the street now, the party's just beginning
The music's playing a celebration song
Under the street lights the scene is being set
A night for romance, a night you won't forget. So
Come join the fun, this ain't no time to be staying at home
The Moulin Rough is going on, yeah
Tonight is gonna be a night like you've never known
We're gonna have a good time the whole night long.
Oh yeah.

YOUR SONG

WORDS & MUSIC BY ELTON JOHN AND BERNIE TAUPIN

My gift is my so - ng, and this one's for you. And you can tell eve - ry - bo - dy,

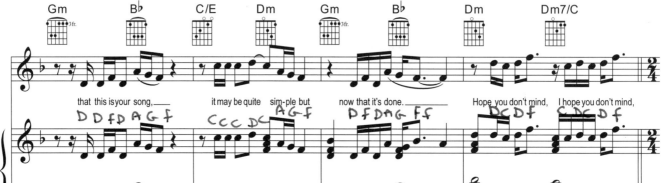

that this is your song, it may be quite sim-ple but now that it's done. Hope you don't mind, I hope you don't mind,

that I put down in words how won-der-ful life is, now you're in the world.

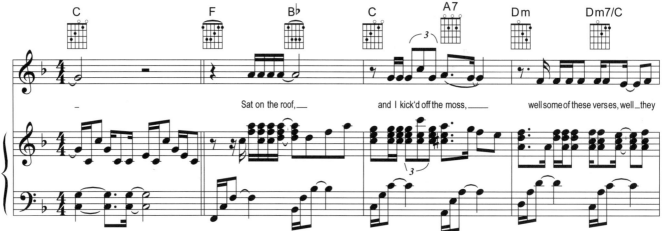

Sat on the roof, and I kick'd off the moss, well some of these verses, well they

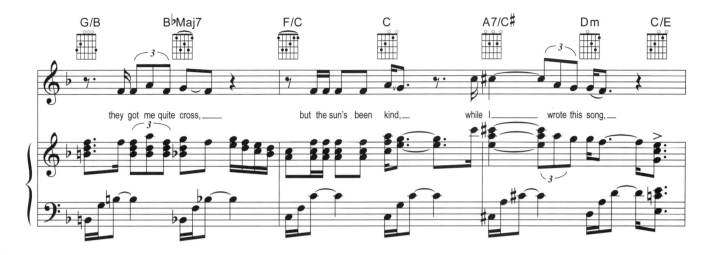

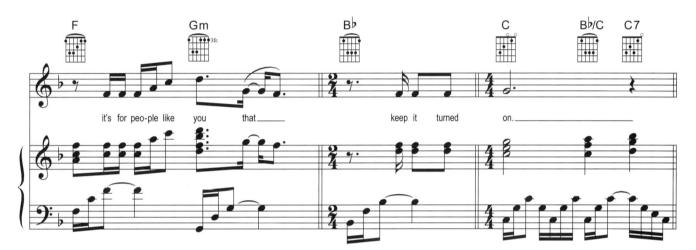

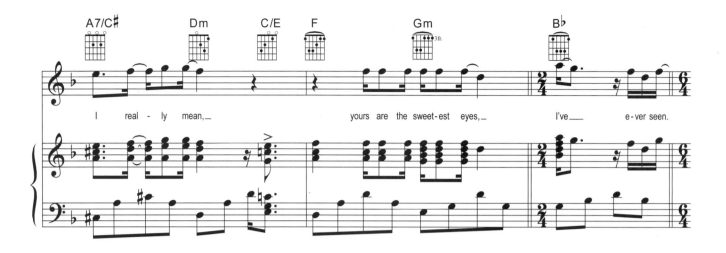

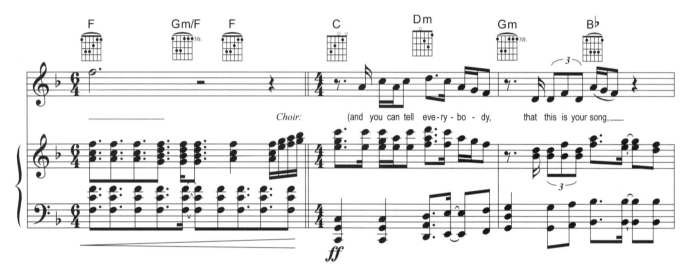

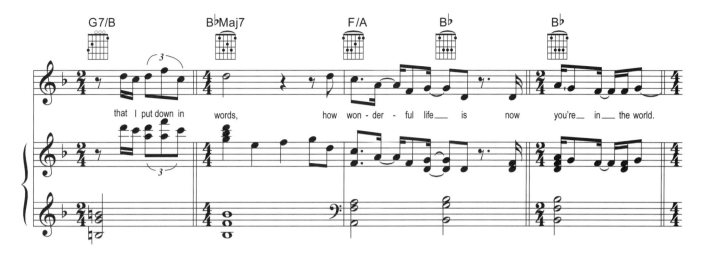

that I put down in words, how won-der-ful life___ is now you're___ in___ the world.

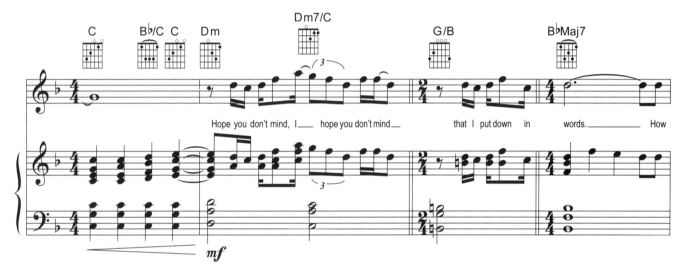

Hope you don't mind, I___ hope you don't mind___ that I put down in words._____ How

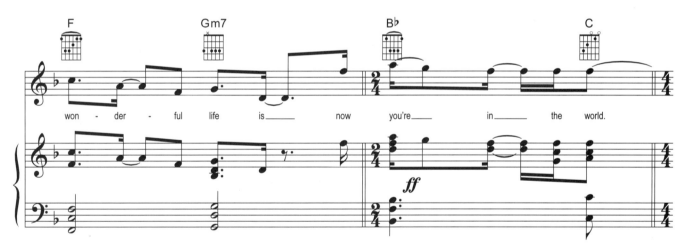

won-der-ful life is___ now you're___ in___ the world.

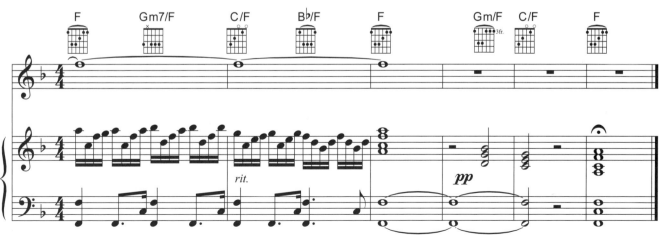

CHILDREN OF THE REVOLUTION

WORDS & MUSIC BY MARC BOLAN

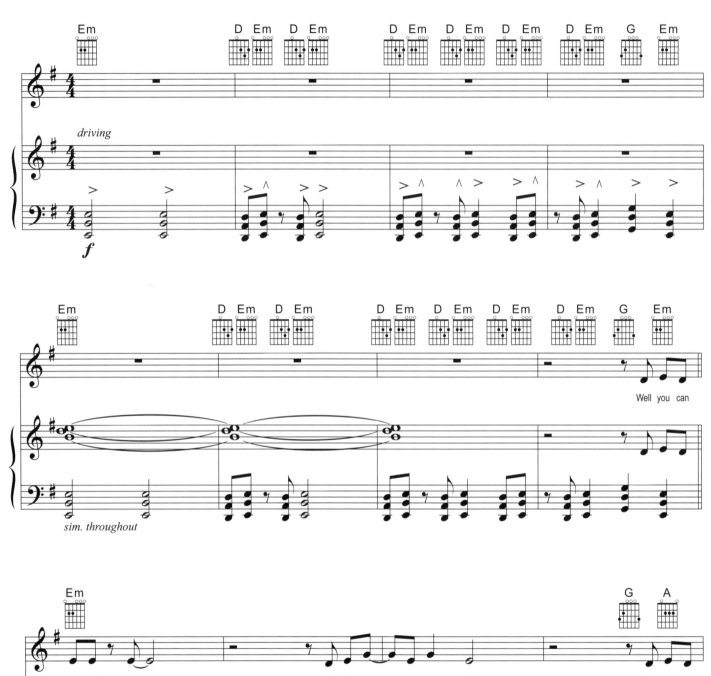

twist and shout, let it all___ hang out. But you

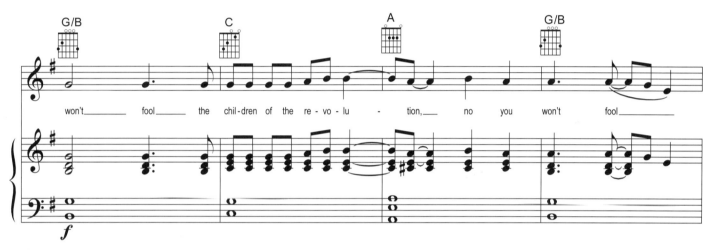

won't___ fool___ the chil-dren of the re-vo-lu - tion,___ no you won't fool___

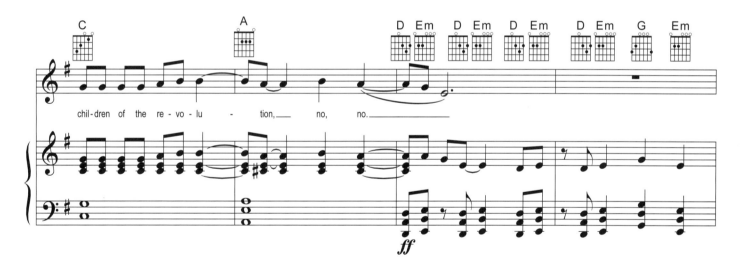

chil-dren of the re-vo-lu - tion,___ no, no.___

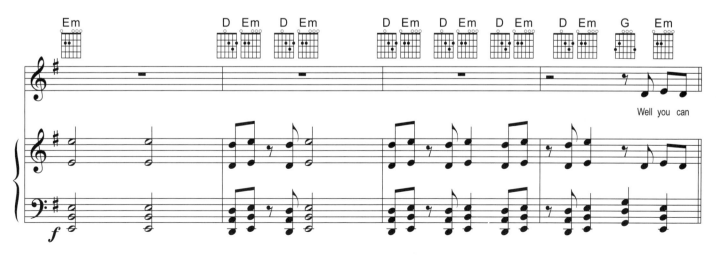

Well you can

tell I play, _____ in the fall - ing rain, _____ I drive a

Rolls _____ Royce, _____ 'cause it's good _____ for my voice. _____ But you

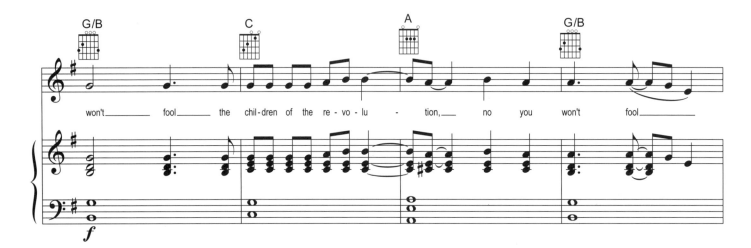

won't _____ fool _____ the chil-dren of the re-vo-lu - tion, _____ no you won't fool _____

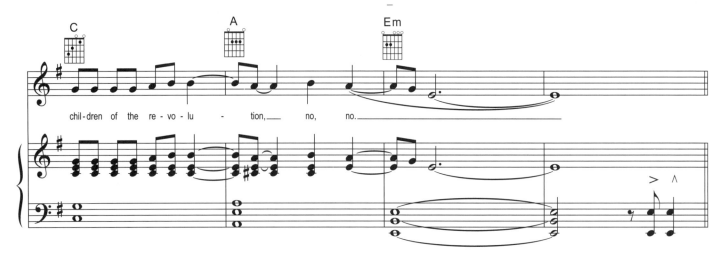

chil-dren of the re-vo-lu - tion, _____ no, no. _____

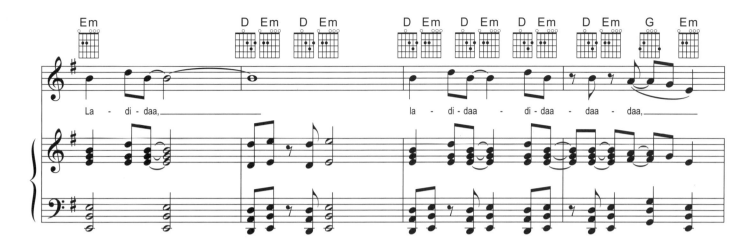

La - di -daa,_____ la - di -daa - di -daa - daa - daa,_____

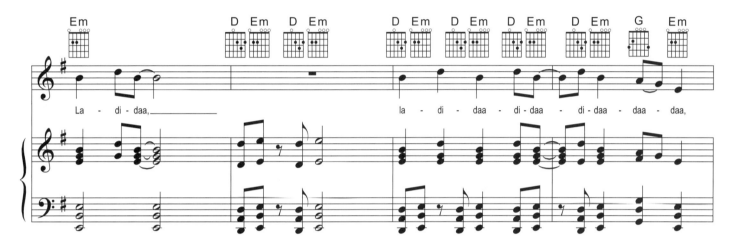

La - di -daa,_____ la - di - daa - di - daa - di - daa - daa - daa,

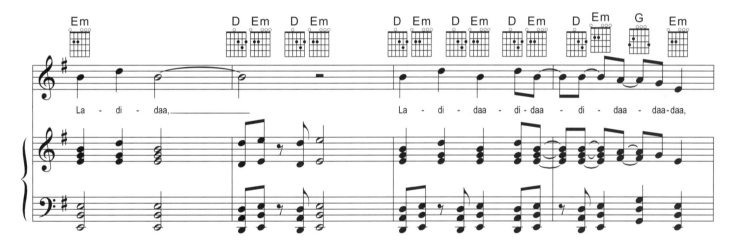

La - di - daa,_____ La - di - daa - di - daa - di - daa - daa-daa,

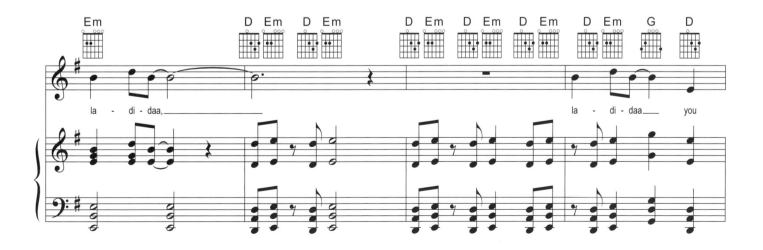

la - di - daa,_____ la - di -daa____ you

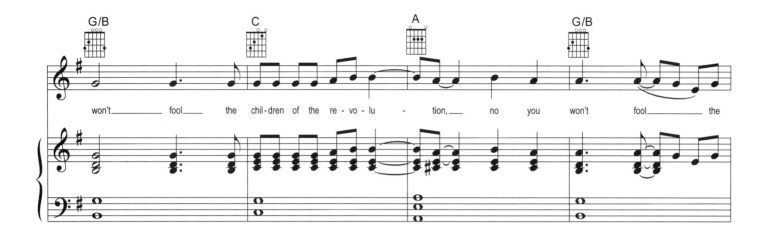

won't_____ fool_____ the chil-dren of the re - vo - lu - tion,_____ no you won't fool_____ the

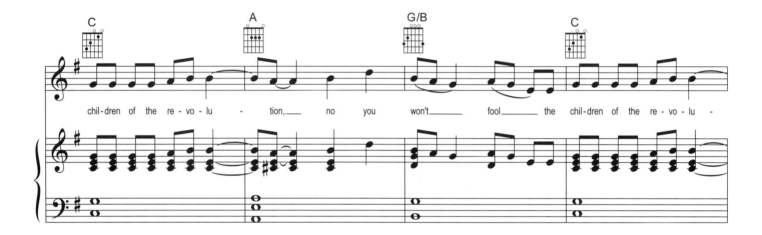

chil-dren of the re - vo - lu - tion,_____ no you won't_____ fool_____ the chil-dren of the re - vo - lu -

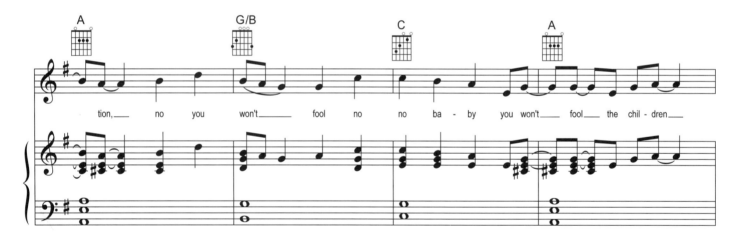

tion,_____ no you won't_____ fool no no ba - by you won't_____ fool____ the chil - dren_____

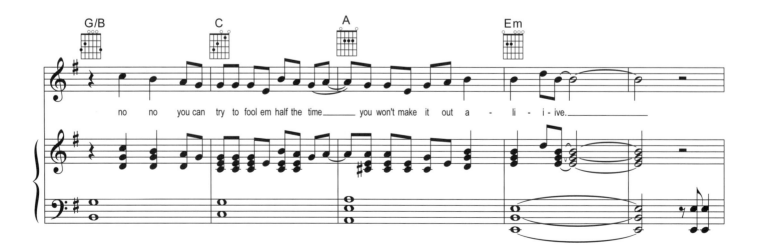

no no you can try to fool em half the time_____ you won't make it out a - li - i - ive._____

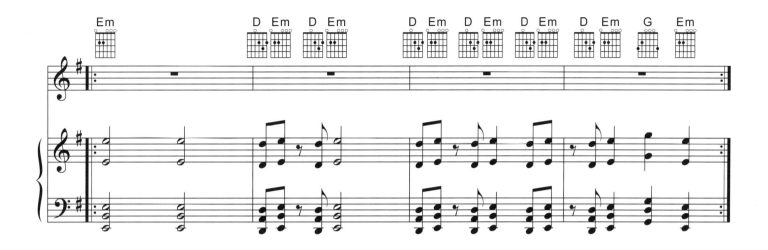

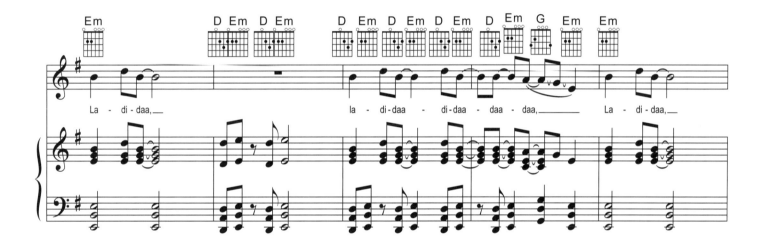

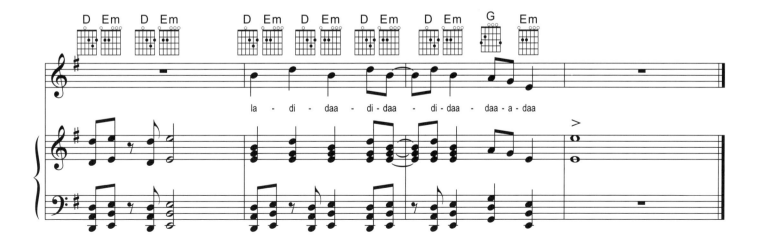

ONE DAY I'LL FLY AWAY

WORDS BY WILL JENNINGS, MUSIC BY JOE SAMPLE

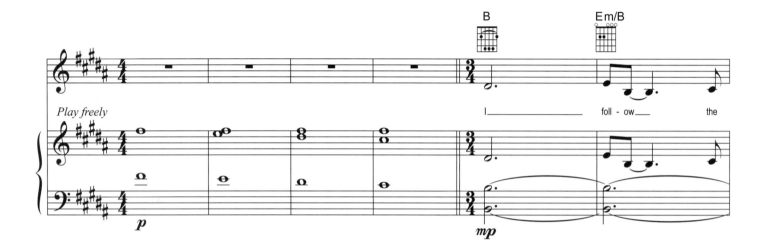

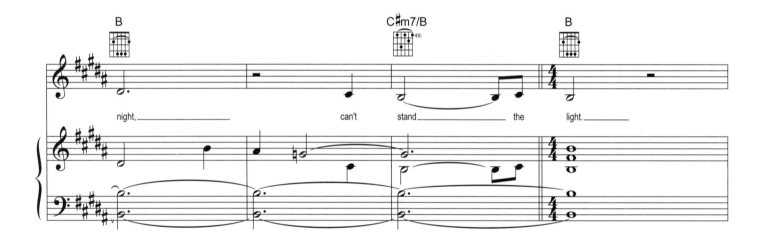

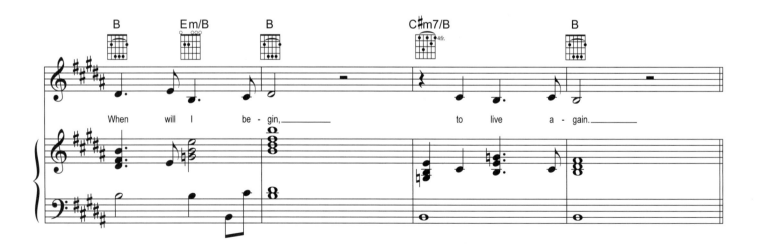

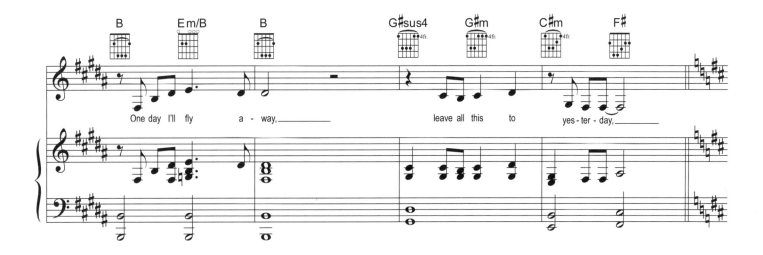

One day I'll fly a-way,_____ leave all this to yes-ter-day,_____

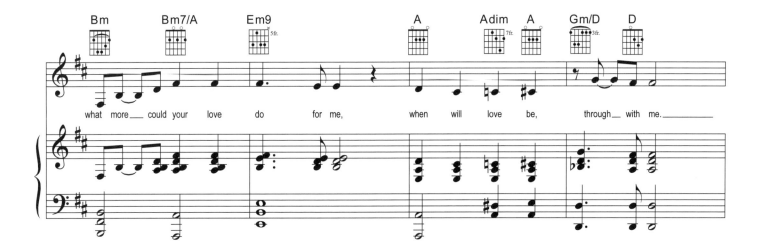

what more___ could your love do for me, when will love be, through___ with me._____

Why live life from dream to dream, and dread the day, when

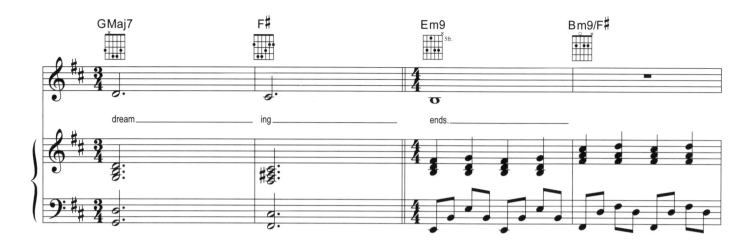

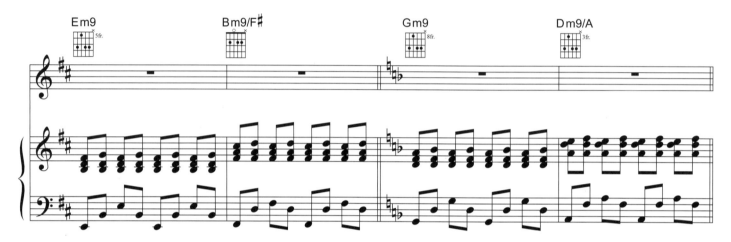

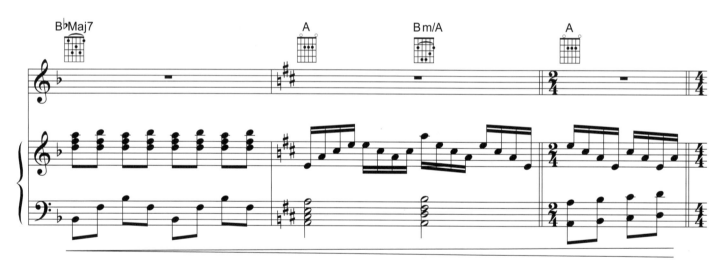

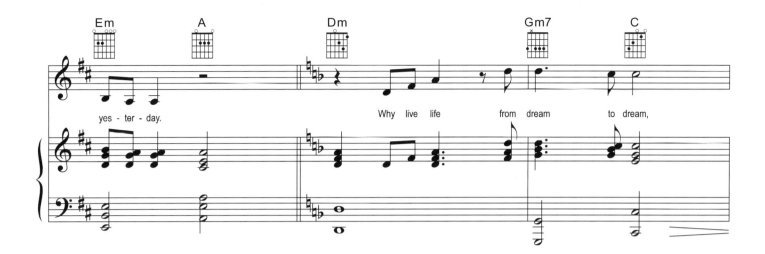

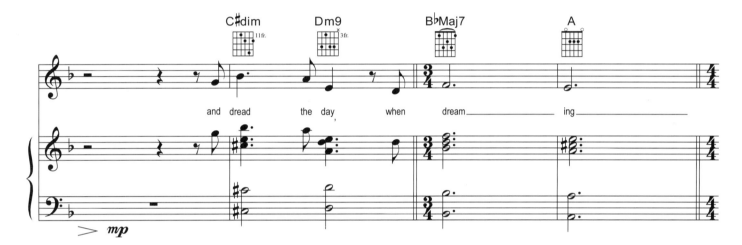

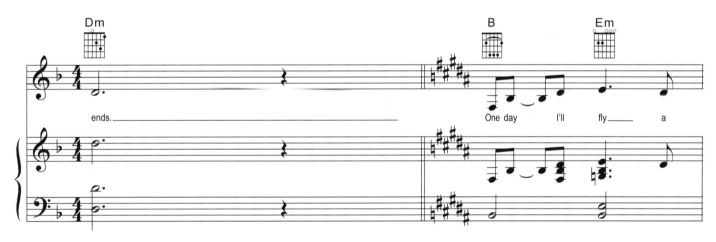

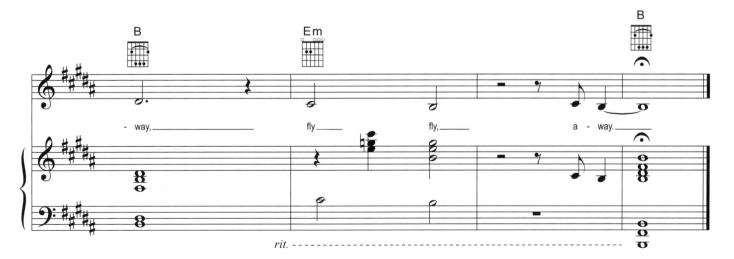

DIAMOND DOGS

WORDS & MUSIC BY DAVID BOWIE

Gm

1. As they pulled you out___ of the ox - y - gen tent___ we'll
(Verse 2 see block lyric)

F6

ask for the lat - est par - ty___ with the si - li - cone___ hump___ and your

Em7(♭5)

Gm

ten inch stump___ just like a priest you was Tod Brown-ing's freak you was

F6

crawl-ing down the al - ley on your hands and your knees.___ I'm sure you're not pro - tect - ed for it's

49

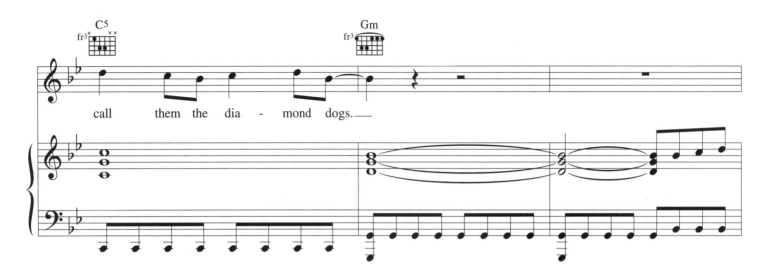

call them the dia - mond dogs.___

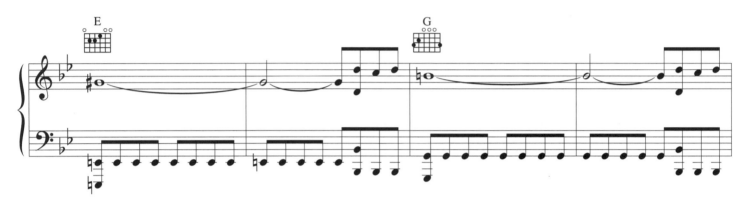

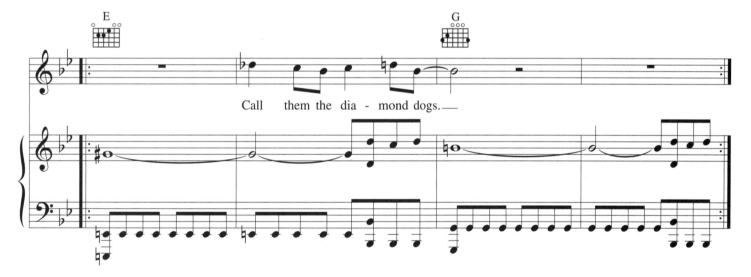

Call them the dia - mond dogs.

Verse 2:

In the year of the scavenger, the season of the bitch
Sashay on the boardwalk, scurry to the ditch
Just another future-song, lonely little kitsch
There's gonna be sorrow try and wake up tomorrow for
Hallowe'en Jack is a real cool cat
He lives on top of Manhattan Chase
The elevator's broke so he slides down the rope
On to the street below, oh Tarzan go man go.

Here they come *etc.*

ELEPHANT LOVE MEDLEY

SEE PAGE 88 FOR COMPLETE SONG TITLES AND WRITER/COPYRIGHT DETAILS

see ____ it is-n't so. *(Spoken:* Oh, no!) Some peo-ple wan-na fill the world ____ with sil-ly

love songs. Well, what's wrong with that, ____ I'd like to know? ____ 'Cause

poco rit.

♩= 150

here I go, ____ girl! ____

Love lifts us up ____ where we be - long, ____ where

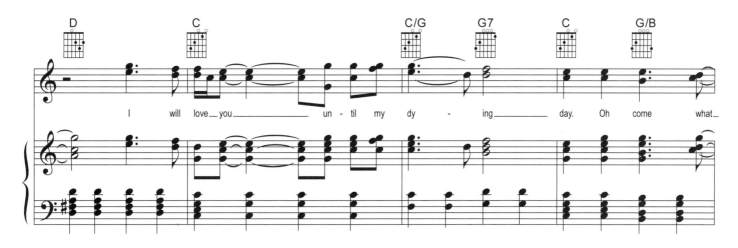

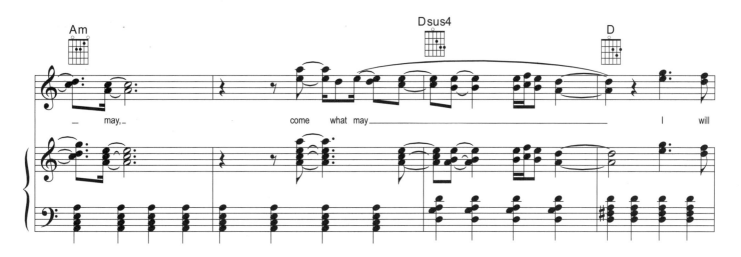

love _____ you _____ will love you   su - dden - ly the world   seems such a per - fect place. ___

Come what _____ may, _____   come what _

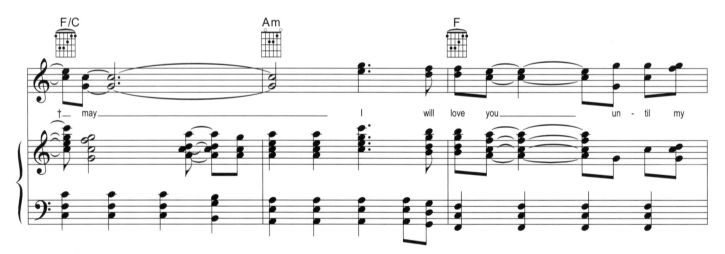

† _ may _____   I   will love you _____   un - til my

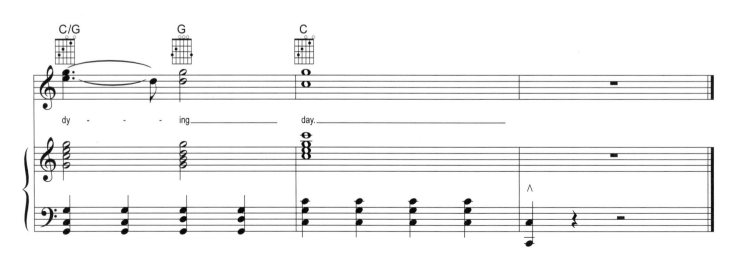

dy - - ing _____ day.

EL TANGO DE ROXANNE

SEE PAGE 88 FOR COMPLETE SONG TITLES AND WRITER/COPYRIGHT DETAILS

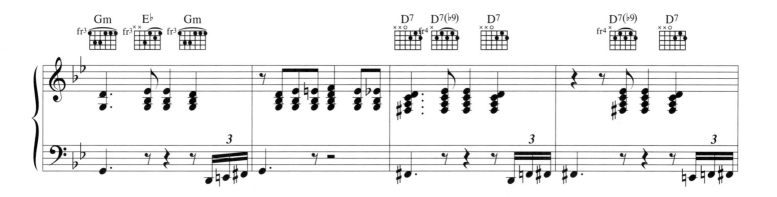

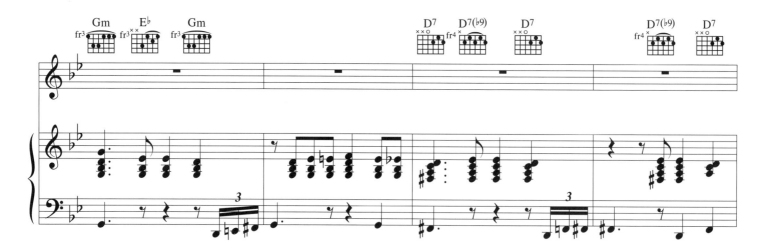

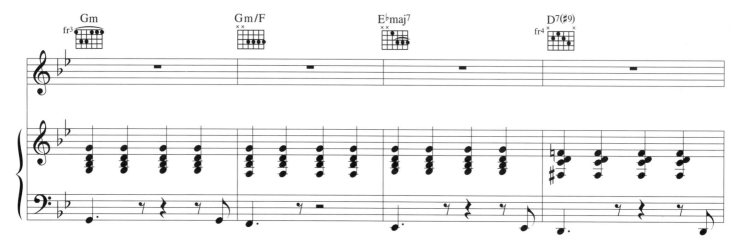

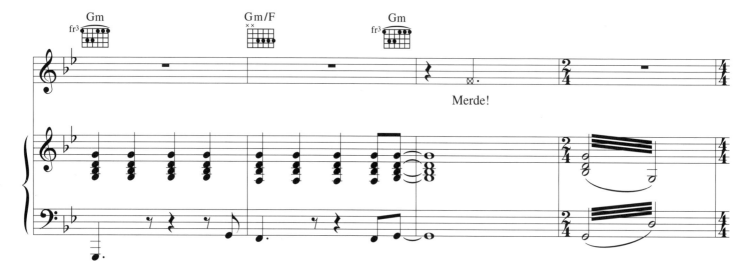

Merde!

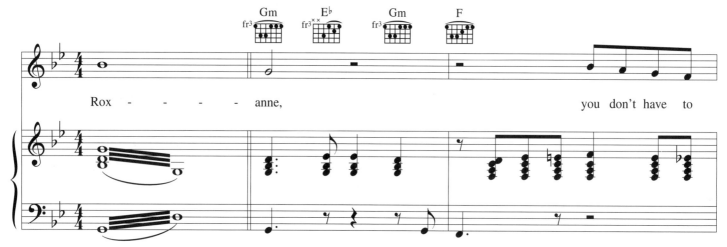

Rox - - - anne,   you don't have to

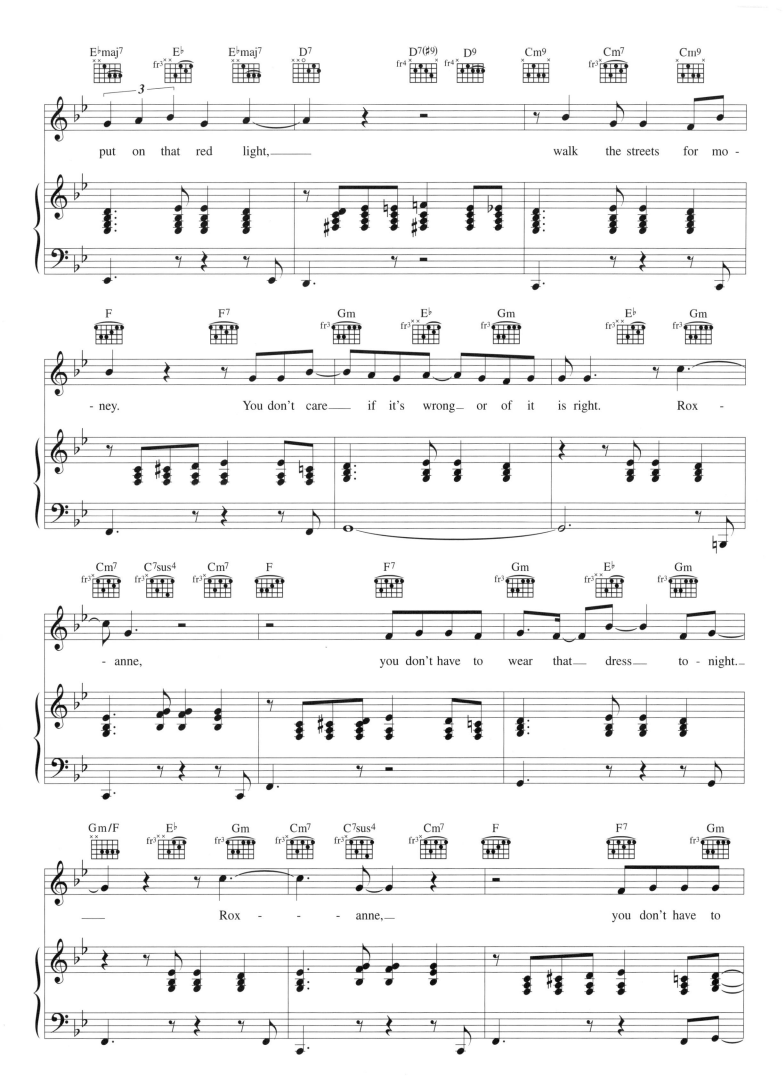

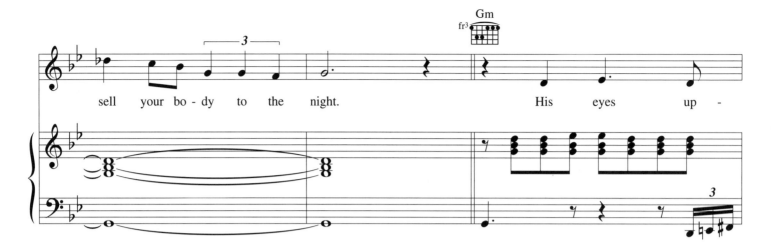

sell your bo-dy to the night. His eyes up -

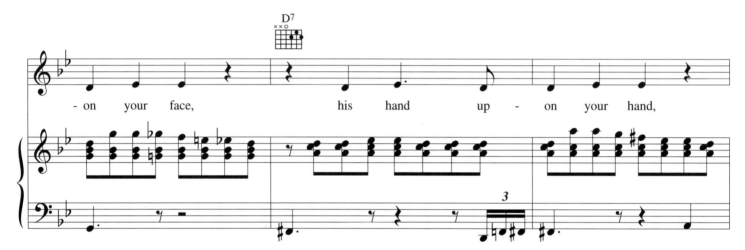

- on your face, his hand up - on your hand,

his lips car-ess your skin; it's more than

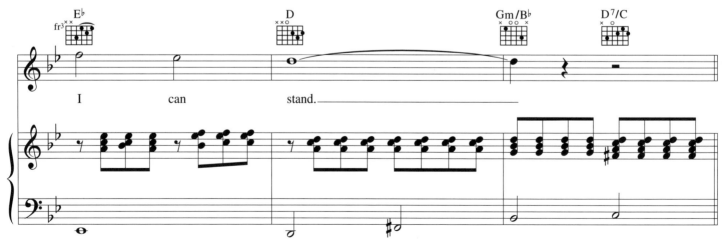

I can stand.

please,   be - lieve me when I   say   I   love___ you.

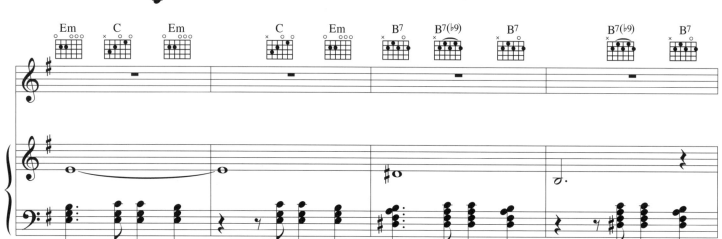

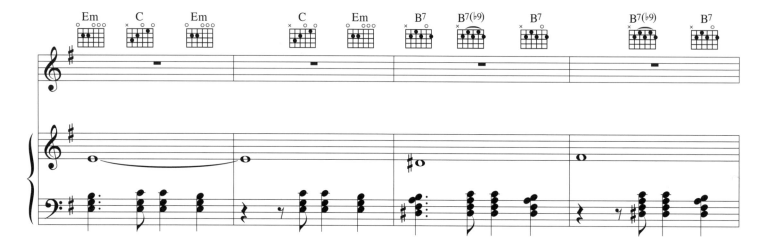

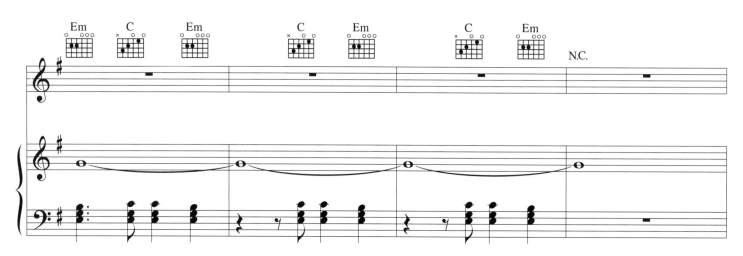

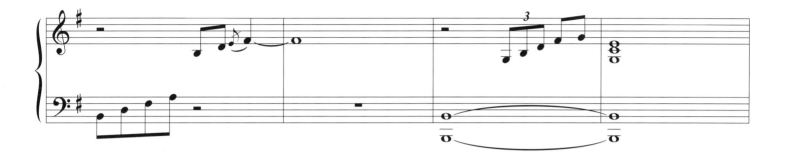

Why　　　does　　　my　　　heart

cry　　　feel - - - ings　　I

can't　　　fight?　　　Why

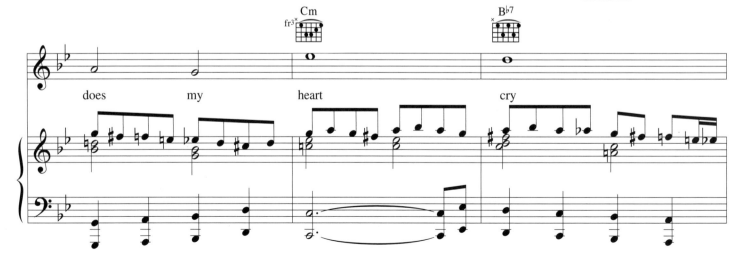

does　　　my　　　heart　　　cry

COMPLAINTE DE LA BUTTE

MUSIC BY GEORGES VAN PARYS, WORDS BY JEAN RENOIR
ENGLISH TRANSLATION BY BERNADETTE COLOMINE

1. La lu-ne trop blême pose un di-a-
(Verse 2 see block lyric)

-dème sur tes che-veux roux._____ La

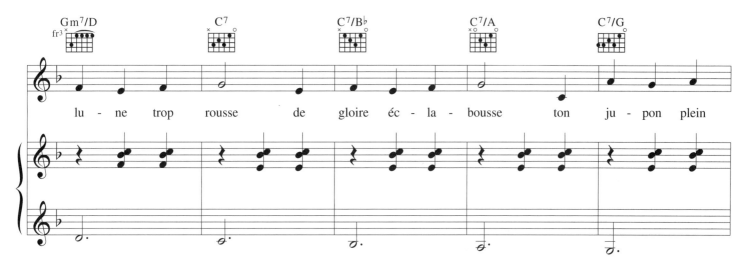

lu - ne trop rousse de gloire éc - la - bousse ton ju - pon plein

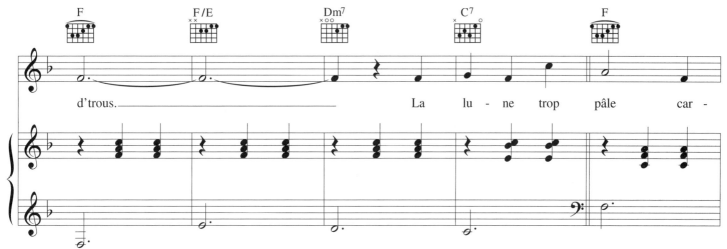

d'trous._____ La lu - ne trop pâle car -

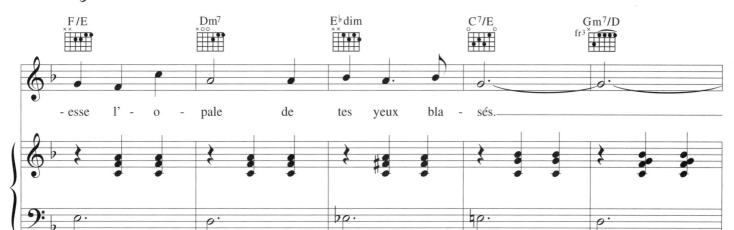

- esse l' - o - pale de tes yeux bla - sés._____

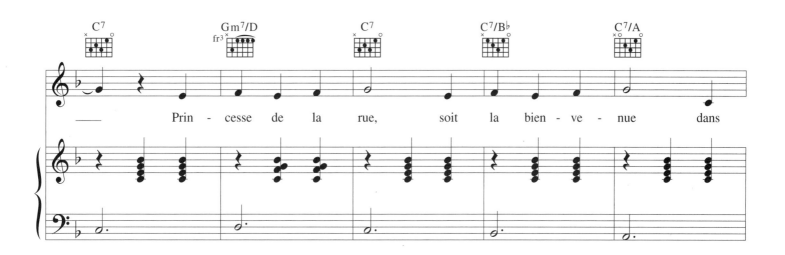

Prin - cesse de la rue, soit la bien - ve - nue dans

mon coeur bles - sé._____ The stair - ways

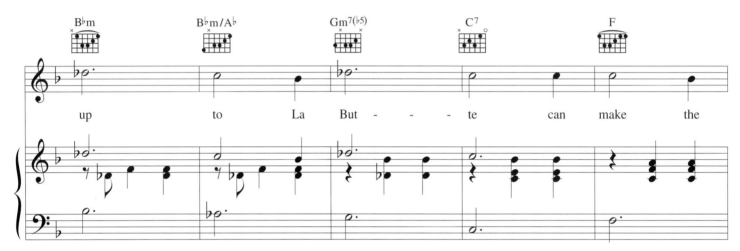

up to La But - - te can make the

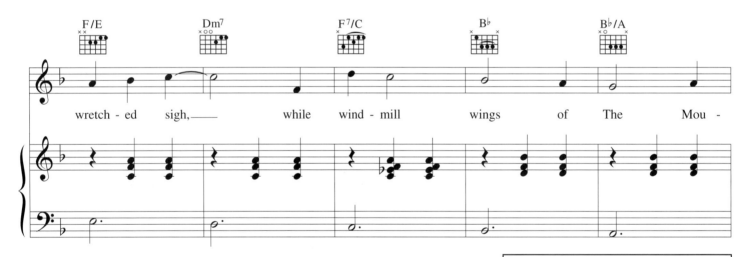

wretch - ed sigh,____ while wind - mill wings of The Mou -

1.

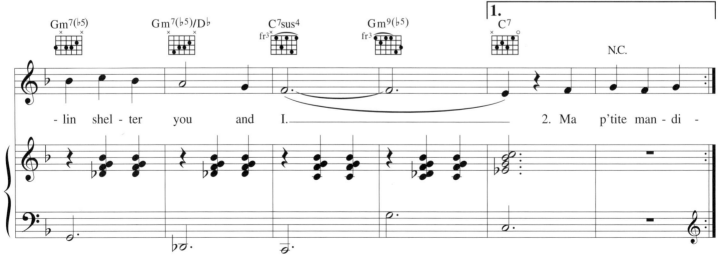

- lin shel - ter you and I._____ 2. Ma p'tite man - di -

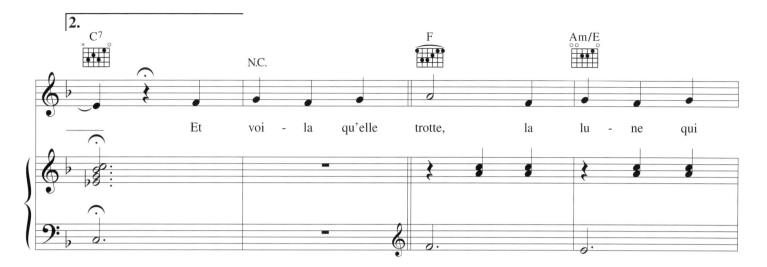

Et voi - la qu'elle trotte, la lu - ne qui

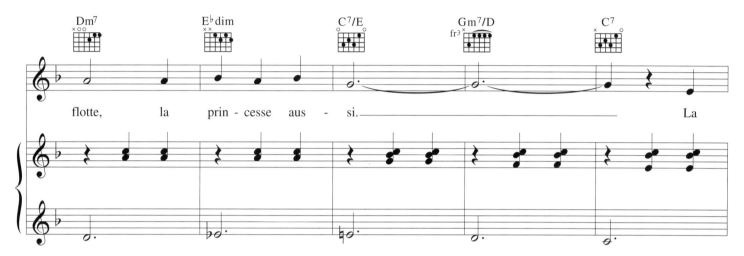

flotte, la prin - cesse aus - si. _____ La

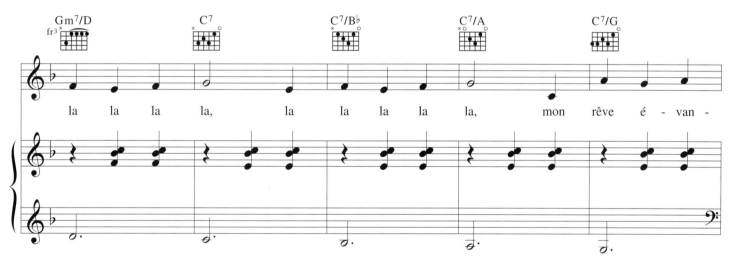

la la la la, la la la la la, mon rêve é - van -

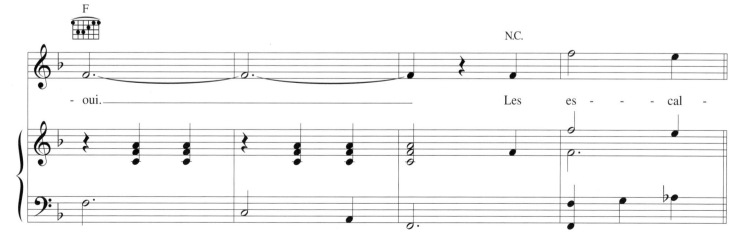

- oui. _____ Les es - - cal -

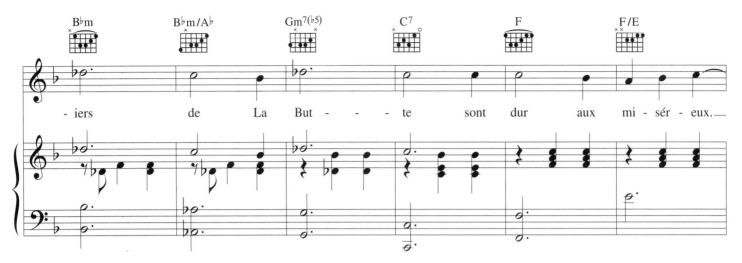

-iers de La But - - - te sont dur aux mi-sér - eux. ___

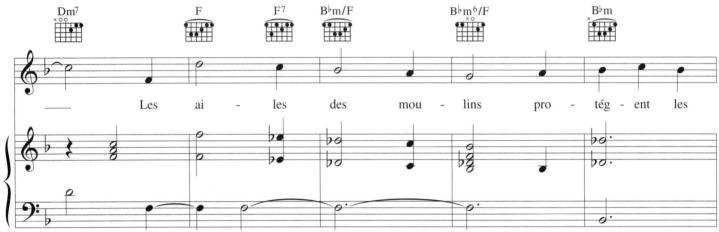

___ Les ai - les des mou - lins pro - tég - ent les

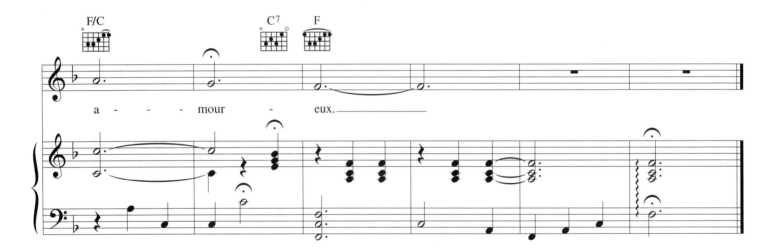

a - - -mour - eux.___

Verse 2:
Ma petite mandigote
Je sens ta menotte
Qui cherche ma main
Je sens ta poitrine
Et ta taille fine
J'oublie mon chagrin.
Je sens sur tes lèvres
Une odeur de fièvre
De gosse mal nourri
Et sous ta caresse
Je sens une ivresse
Qui m'anéantit.

HINDI SAD DIAMONDS

SEE PAGE 88 FOR COMPLETE SONG TITLES AND WRITER/COPYRIGHT DETAILS

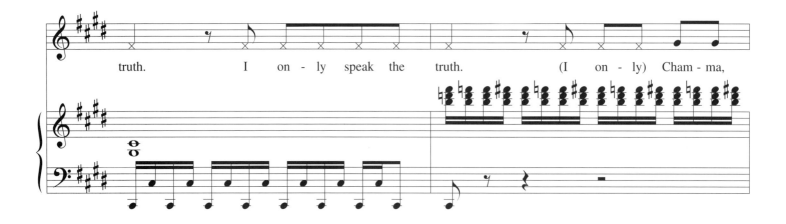

ay - e - ay - e - a.   Ny nay e nay e ay.   Cham - ma,

cham - ma,   ay cham - ma,— cham - ma,   cham - ma,—

cham - ma.   *etc. ad lib. vocal*

Ni_____ ni sho__ no

sa sho kays oh ni, sa sho kays ah na ja.

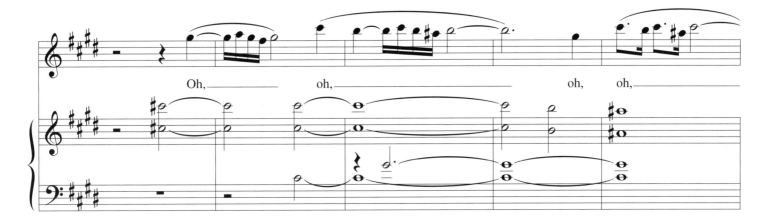

Oh,_____ oh,_____ oh, oh,_____

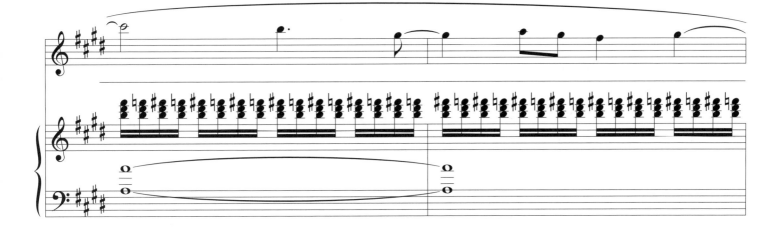

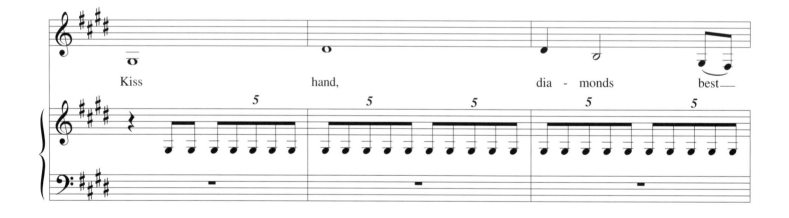

dia - monds best_ friend.___ Men

cold girls_____

old. And we all lose our

optional add octave

charms_____ in the end._____

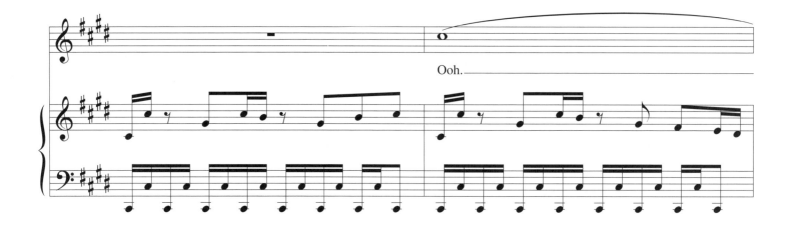

Ooh.

Dia - monds are a,

dia - monds are a, dia - monds are a,

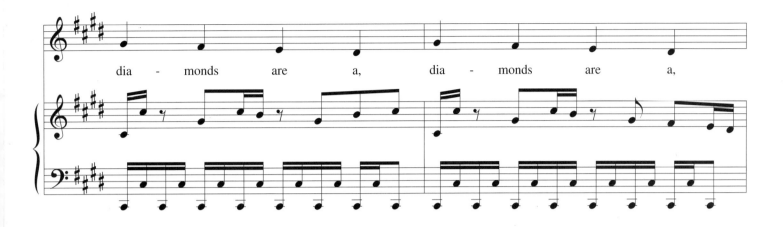

dia - monds are a, dia - monds are a,

molto rit.

dia - monds are a, dia - monds are a____

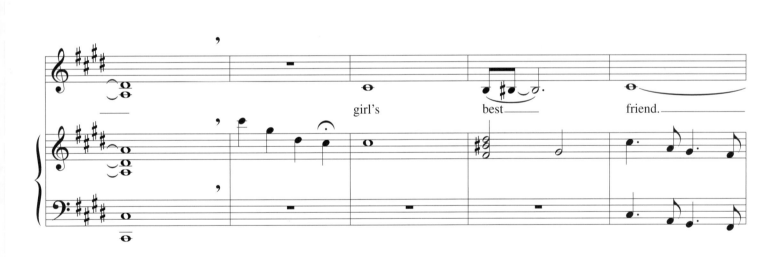

____ girl's best____ friend.____

____ *Spoken:* She is mine   She is mine

1/02 (42450)

Exclusive Distributors:
Music Sales Limited, 8/9 Frith Street, London W1D 3JB, England.
Music Sales Pty Limited, 120 Rothschild Avenue, Rosebery, NSW 2018, Australia.

Order No. AM972763 ISBN 0-7119-9204-5
This book © Copyright 2001 by Wise Publications.

Music arranged by Sean Peter and Jack Long.
Music processed by Paul Ewers Music Design.
Printed in the United Kingdom by Caligraving Limited, Thetford, Norfolk.

Music Sales' complete catalogue describes thousands of titles and is
available in full colour sections by subject, direct from Music Sales Limited.
Please state your areas of interest and send a cheque/postal order
for £1.50 for postage to: Music Sales Limited,
Newmarket Road, Bury St. Edmunds, Suffolk IP33 3YB.

www.musicsales.com

Your Guarantee of Quality:
As publishers, we strive to produce every book to the
highest commercial standards. This book matches the running
order of the original album. It has been carefully designed to
minimise awkward page turns and to make playing from it
a real pleasure. Particular care has been given to specifying acid-free,
neutral-sized paper made from pulps which have not been elemental
chlorine bleached. This pulp is from farmed sustainable forests
and was produced with special regard for the environment.
Throughout, the printing and binding have been planned to ensure
a sturdy, attractive publication which should give years of enjoyment.
If your copy fails to meet our high standards, please inform us and
we will gladly replace it.

ADDITIONAL CREDITS FOR SONG MEDLEYS: